I Wonder How God Hears Me

Mona Gansberg Hodgson

Illustrated by Chris Sharp

CPH

SAINT LOUIS

*With thanks to all who have had a part in teaching me
about the power of prayer*

I Wonder Series

I Wonder How Fish Sleep
I Wonder Who Hung the Moon in the Sky
I Wonder Who Stretched the Giraffe's Neck
I Wonder How God Made Me
I Wonder What I Can Give God

Scripture quotations, unless otherwise indicated, are taken from the Good News Bible, the Bible in TODAY'S ENGLISH VERSION. Copyright © Amercian Bible Society, 1966, 1971, 1976. Used by permission.

Text copyright © 1999 Mona Gansberg Hodgson
Art copyright © 1999 Concordia Publishing House
Published by Concordia Publishing House
3558 S. Jefferson Avenue, St. Louis, MO 63118-3968
Manufactured in the United States of America

2   3   4   5   6   7   8   9   10   08   07   06   05   04   03   02   01

A Note to Parents and Teachers

The *I Wonder Series* will delight children while helping them grow in their understanding and appreciation of God. Readers will discover biblical truths through the experiences and whimsy of 7-year-old Jared.

I Wonder How God Hears Me assures children that God cares about them and hears their prayers. Jared provides a playful exploration of how God hears His children. In the end, Jared and the readers learn that God personally knows them and hears their prayers just as God knows what is in their hearts.

The activities on pages 30–32 will help children apply and practice the truths revealed in Jared's imaginative investigation of how God hears him. Enjoy!

You know everything I do; from far away You understand all my thoughts. Even before I speak, You already know what I will say (Psalm 139:2 & 4).

Mona Gansberg Hodgson

Hi! My name is Jared.
I live in Arizona.

Do you ever
wonder about
things? I do.

Everything I hear makes me
wonder. Noises make me
wonder. People's voices make me
wonder. Do you like to wonder? I do.

When Papa Ray
thanked God for our
lunch today, I began to
wonder. God has a lot of
people to listen to. How
does He hear me?

How does
God hear you? I wonder.
Do you wonder too?

When my mom sings in church she uses a microphone so everyone can hear her. I wonder if there are

microphones all around us so God can hear us when we talk to Him. What do you think?

Our stereo has speakers that help us hear singing and talking on the radio. Our computer has speakers too. Do you think God

has speakers in heaven to help Him hear us when we pray? I wonder.

My dad showed me Psalm 116:2 in the Bible. It says God turns His ear to us. God is so amazing! He doesn't need microphones or speakers to hear us when we pray.

11

Papa Ray is getting old. He puts a hearing aid into his ear to help him hear.

The Bible says that God was here even before the beginning of the world. That makes God really old. Do you think God needs a hearing aid to help Him hear us when we pray? I wonder.

Papa Ray read Hebrews 13:8 to me. It says that God is the same yesterday and today and forever. That means God doesn't grow old or ever need a hearing aid. God can always hear our prayers.

My little sister takes a nap every day. She gets tired and falls asleep.

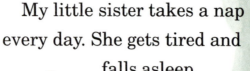

Does God get tired

and take a nap? If God is asleep, how will He hear me when I pray? I wonder.

My dad says that Psalm 121:3 tells us that God doesn't sleep. He never needs to take a nap. If God is always awake, then He can always hear our prayers.

God is amazing!

15

I can count to three in Spanish. Uno. Dos. Tres. And I can say some words in Swahili too. "Rafiki" means "friend" in Swahili. Would God understand me if I talked to Him in a different language? I wonder.

Papa Ray says Jesus spoke to God the Father in Hebrew. God knows every language and understands them all. Wow! God can hear our prayers in any language.

17

When my cousin grew, his voice changed. If my voice changed, would God still recognize it and hear my prayers? I wonder. What do you think?

← my Cousin

My mom showed me Psalm 139 in the Bible. In the first verse, David says God knows him very well. That means God knows us very well too. He can hear our prayers even if our voice changes. Amazing!

19

One time my dad had a sore throat and laryngitis. He couldn't talk for a whole day.

What if I had laryngitis and I couldn't talk? Would God hear me then?

How would God hear me if I couldn't speak? I wonder.

Thanks for the soup, Sparky.

21

Car Wash

Yesterday at the car wash I saw a girl using her hands to talk to her mother. Papa Ray said the girl was deaf. She couldn't hear words. She used her hands to make words in a special language called "sign language."

Do you think God hears us when we use sign language? I wonder.

My mom told me about
1 Samuel 16:7. It's a verse in the
Bible that says our heart shows
God what we're feeling and
thinking. God knows what we're
trying to say even before we say
it. That means God can understand our prayers even if we
have laryngitis or when we use
sign language. God is so
amazing!

I know God doesn't need a microphone, a speaker, or a hearing aid to hear me. I know God can hear me when I whisper or speak in another language or when I use my hands to talk to Him.

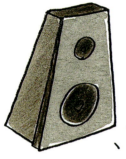

God can hear me thinking about Him and thanking Him even when

I'm not using my voice or my hands. God is so-o-o amazing!

27

I like to wonder, don't you?

When I wonder I like to think about God. I like to thank God for caring about me and for hearing me when I pray. I thank God for hearing the thoughts I think and the words I whisper in my heart. I thank God for knowing all my needs, especially my need for His love. After all, He loves me so much that He sent Jesus as my Savior.

Thank You, God, for caring about me.

**Thank You, God, for knowing my needs
and hearing my prayers.**

**Thank You for being my amazing God!
For Jesus' sake. Amen.**

*You know everything I do; from far away You
understand all my thoughts. Even before I speak,
You already know what I will say (Psalm 139:2 & 4).*

36

31

What do you like to talk to God about? Tell me about it in the space below.